CYPRUS

...in Pictures

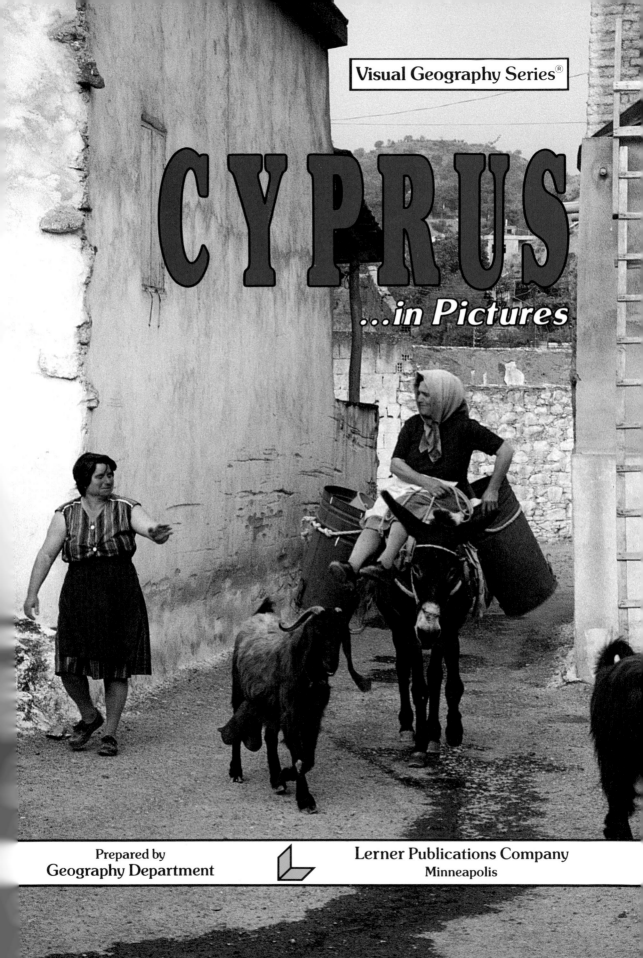

Visual Geography Series®

CYPRUS

...in Pictures

Prepared by
Geography Department

Lerner Publications Company
Minneapolis

Independent Picture Service

Cypriot farmers pick and crate oranges for shipment abroad.

This book is a newly commissioned title in the Visual Geography Series. The text is set in 10/12 Century Textbook.

LIBRARY OF CONGRESS CATALOGING-IN-PUBLICATION DATA

Cyprus in pictures / prepared by Geography Department, Lerner Publications Company.
    p. cm. — (Visual geography series)
Includes index.
    Summary: Describes the topography, history, society, economy, and governmental structure of Cyprus.
    ISBN 0-8225-1910-0 (lib. bdg.)
    1. Cyprus. [1. Cyprus.] I. Lerner Publications Company. II. Series: Visual geography series (Minneapolis, Minn.)
DS54.A3C97   1992
956.45—dc   91-43188
                          CIP
                          AC

International Standard Book Number: 0-8225-1910-0
Library of Congress Catalog Card Number: 91-43188

VISUAL GEOGRAPHY SERIES®

Publisher
Harry Jonas Lerner
Associate Publisher
Nancy M. Campbell
Senior Editor
Mary M. Rodgers
Editors
Gretchen Bratvold
Tom Streissguth
Assistant Editor
Colleen Sexton
Photo Researcher
Bill Kauffmann
Editorial/Photo Assistants
Anne Campbell
Marybeth Campbell
Consultants/Contributors
Miltos Miltiades
Sandra K. Davis
Designer
Jim Simondet
Cartographer
Carol F. Barrett
Indexers
Kristine S. Schubert
Sylvia Timian
Production Manager
Gary J. Hansen

Independent Picture Service

Soldiers stand guard outside the massive walls of Kyrenia, on the northern coast of Cyprus.

Acknowledgments

Title page photo © Andrew E. Beswick.

Elevation contours adapted from *The Times Atlas of the World*, seventh comprehensive edition (New York: Times Books, 1985).

1 2 3 4 5 6 97 96 95 94 93 92

The port of Kyrenia lies between the Kyrenia Mountains and the Mediterranean Sea. A fortress dating to the thirteenth century rises above the entrance to Kyrenia's harbor.

Contents

Introduction **7**

1) The Land **10**
Topography. Rivers and Lakes. Climate. Flora and Fauna. Natural Resources. Cities.

2) History and Government **20**
Egyptian and Greek Settlement. Middle Eastern Realms. The Ptolemaic Kings. Roman Rule and Christianity. Byzantine Cyprus. The Lusignan Kings. The Ottoman Conquest. Mediterranean Conflicts. The World Wars. Independence. Recent Events. Government.

3) The People **39**
Religion and Festivals. Health and Education. Language and Literature. The Arts. Recreation and Food.

4) The Economy **50**
Manufacturing. Agriculture. Trade. Mining and Energy. Tourism. Transportation. The Future.

Index **64**

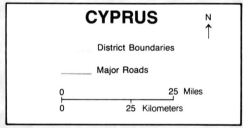

CYPRUS

N

District Boundaries

—————— Major Roads

0   25 Miles

0   25 Kilometers

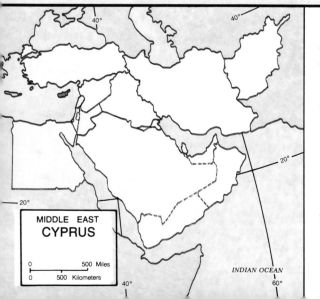

MIDDLE EAST
CYPRUS

0   500 Miles

0   500 Kilometers

METRIC CONVERSION CHART
To Find Approximate Equivalents

WHEN YOU KNOW:	MULTIPLY BY:	TO FIND:
AREA		
acres	0.41	hectares
square miles	2.59	square kilometers
CAPACITY		
gallons	3.79	liters
LENGTH		
feet	30.48	centimeters
yards	0.91	meters
miles	1.61	kilometers
MASS (weight)		
pounds	0.45	kilograms
tons	0.91	metric tons
VOLUME		
cubic yards	0.77	cubic meters
TEMPERATURE		
degrees Fahrenheit	0.56 (*after* subtracting 32)	degrees Celsius

According to legend, the rocky cape of Petra tou Romiou was the birthplace of Aphrodite, the Greek goddess of love. At the city of Old Paphos, a few miles to the northwest, the ancient Cypriots built a temple to Aphrodite.

Introduction

Cyprus, an island in the eastern Mediterranean Sea, lies at a historic crossroads of trade and culture. Although it is a small land mass, Cyprus has attracted settlers from Africa, the Middle East, and Europe for more than 3,000 years. Cypriots have benefited from the island's natural resources, favorable climate, and strategic location. But Cyprus has also suffered foreign invasions, economic decline, and civil conflict.

The earliest inhabitants of Cyprus sailed to the island from Asia Minor (modern Turkey) and the Middle East. Hunting and farming supported prehistoric villagers who lived along the coast and in Cyprus's mountain valleys. Mycenaeans from southern Greece, who arrived about 1500 B.C., built ports on the southern coast and imported the Greek language, culture, and religion. Although the ancient kingdoms of Assyria, Egypt, and Persia conquered and ruled Cyprus during the next thousand years, the thriving ports of Cyprus remained Greek.

Many other peoples have settled on Cyprus since ancient times. For example, Phoenicians from what is now Lebanon established cities and ports in southern Cyprus after the arrival of the Mycenaeans. In 58 B.C., officials of the growing Roman Empire—which began on the Italian Peninsula—took control of Cyprus's Greek and Phoenician cities. Followers of Christianity, a Middle Eastern religion, arrived in the first century A.D. and converted many Cypriots to their faith. The Ottoman Turks of Asia Minor, who conquered Cyprus in the 1500s, practiced the religion of Islam but permitted Greek-speaking inhabitants of Cyprus to remain Christians.

For three centuries, while the island was under Ottoman control, Turks settled

Dockworkers load bales of agricultural goods in the busy Cypriot port of Limassol.

farms and villages on Cyprus. Although they lived side by side, the Greek- and Turkish-speaking Cypriots were separated by their languages, religions, and cultures. These differences contributed to a bitter political clash that still divides Greek and Turkish Cypriots.

Cyprus was a possession of Britain from the early twentieth century until 1960. The British developed Cypriot industry and trade, but Cyprus suffered worsening civil conflict under British rule. After independence, Turkish- and Greek-speaking Cypriots still disagreed over the island's future. At the same time, many Greek Cypriots sought to unite Cyprus with the Republic of Greece.

In 1974 Greeks favoring this union overthrew Archbishop Makarios (Mikhail Khristodolou Mouskas), the island's president. This action prompted Turkey to invade northern Cyprus, an event that led to the division of Cyprus into northern (Turkish-speaking) and southern (Greek-speaking) zones. The conflict, which forced both Greek and Turkish Cypriots to flee

Courtesy of Cyprus Tourist Organization, Nicosia

Traditional dancers perform for a gathering of villagers and Eastern Orthodox clergy in southern Cyprus. Most Greek Cypriots are members of the Eastern Orthodox Church.

In northern Cyprus, Turkish soldiers show the flag of Turkey during the conflict that divided the island in the summer of 1974.

Courtesy of Embassy of the Republic of Cyprus

their homes and businesses, also shut down factories, farms, and hotels. Tourism, a mainstay of the Cypriot economy, nearly ceased. Since 1974 two separate administrations have been governing Cyprus, and little communication or movement occurs between the island's northern and southern zones.

Although southern Cyprus has largely recovered from the effects of the 1974 conflict, the economy of northern Cyprus remains stagnant. In addition, relations between Greece and Turkey are strained over the island's future status. Turkish and Greek Cypriots have long expressed a desire to reunite their island. Despite the efforts of European states and the United Nations to bring about reunification, the two sides have not been able to reach an agreement.

In 1974 thousands of Cypriots fled their homes to escape the fierce fighting among Greek and Turkish Cypriots and the Turkish military. These children play in a tent camp set up to house the refugees.

Courtesy of Embassy of the Republic of Cyprus

A twisted tree shades part of the Roman ruins at Soloi in northern Cyprus. Many ancient cities grew along Cyprus's coast, where level land could be irrigated by streams that ran down to the sea from the interior mountains.

1) The Land

Lying in the eastern Mediterranean Sea, the island of Cyprus is 60 miles west of Syria and 40 miles south of Turkey. The nearest Greek territory—250 miles to the west—is the island of Rhodes. Cyprus is 140 miles across at its widest point. The greatest distance from north to south is about 60 miles. The third largest Mediterranean island, Cyprus covers 3,572 square miles—an area that is about half the size of the state of Hawaii.

Cyprus has a winding coastline with many steep capes, narrow inlets, and wide bays. The long and mountainous Karpas Peninsula points to the northeast and ends at Cape Andreas. The island's interior is made up of a wide, flat plain flanked by mountain ranges to the north and south.

Historically, the fertile land, mineral resources, and good harbors on Cyprus have allowed its inhabitants to prosper from agriculture, mining, and trade.

Topography

The lowlands of the Mesaoria Plain stretch across the middle of Cyprus. This fertile region contains farms, pastures, small towns, and villages. The Mesaoria Plain is also the site of Nicosia, the island's capital and largest city. Drought and centuries of intensive farming have left much of the plain bare of vegetation. Short, narrow rivers that flow during winter and spring run into the area from highlands to the north and south, providing water for drinking and for irrigation. To the west, facing Morphou Bay, lies the Morphou Plain.

The steep slopes of the Kyrenia Mountains rise in the northeast and run the length of the Karpas Peninsula. These highlands tower over the coastline on both sides of the peninsula. Small villages, fruit orchards, and the port of Kyrenia lie along a narrow strip of level land between the northern slope of the mountains and the sea.

South of the Mesaoria Plain are the Troodos Mountains. The forested peaks and foothills of the Troodos highlands cover nearly half of Cyprus. In the center of this range rises Mount Olympus (6,406 feet), the highest point on the island. Modern resorts, busy port cities, and the extensive remains of ancient cities dot the coast south of the Troodos Mountains.

Sandy beaches divided by rocky cliffs stretch along Cyprus's southern coast, the site of the ports of Paphos, Larnaca, and

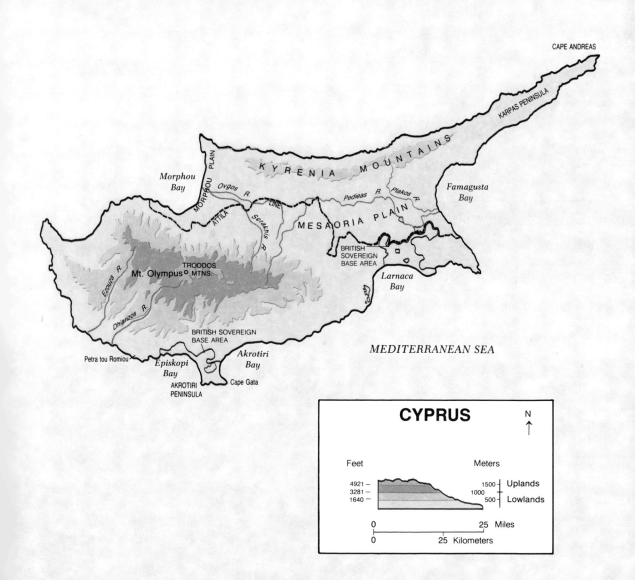

The tenth-century castle of Saint Hilarion clings to a rough peak in the Kyrenia Mountains. Sparse vegetation dots the range, which parallels the northeastern coast of Cyprus.

Limassol. Since Cyprus won its independence in 1960, two British military bases—on Episkopi Bay and on Larnaca Bay—have remained in operation. The Akrotiri Peninsula, which makes up part of a British base, separates Episkopi Bay to the west and Akrotiri Bay to the east. This small peninsula ends at Cape Gata, the southernmost point on the island.

Rivers and Lakes

With limited rainfall and frequent summer droughts, Cyprus has no permanently flowing rivers. During the short rainy season, however, small streams carry rain and melting snow down the lower slopes of the Troodos and Kyrenia mountains. The Ezouza and Dhiarizos rivers are seasonal waterways that run south to the Mediterranean from the heights of the Troodos range.

Seasonal rivers also flow in the Cypriot lowlands. On the Mesaoria Plain, the

Melting snow feeds this short, rushing stream in the Troodos Mountains. Many waterways on Cyprus are seasonal and run dry during the hot summer months.

Ovgos and Serakhis rivers travel north and then west, eventually emptying into Morphou Bay. A dam on the Ovgos provides water to farms and villages in the region. The Pedieas River runs through Nicosia and the central Mesaoria Plain. Paralleling this waterway is the Plakos River, which flows through a wide plain in eastern Cyprus. Both rivers end at Famagusta Bay near the ancient site of Salamis.

Saltwater lakes, which contain water only during the rainy season, fill shallow depressions near the southern coast. The largest of these lakes sits in the center of the Akrotiri Peninsula. Three miles south of Larnaca is a salt lake that lies 10 feet below sea level. Small freshwater lakes also exist in the lowlands west and south of Famagusta, a port on Famagusta Bay.

Climate

Like many other Mediterranean countries, Cyprus has dry, hot summers and rainy, mild winters. Winds that blow from the west lessen the summer heat, and humidity remains low throughout the year. Some coastal towns enjoy as many as 340 days of sunshine per year. The rainy season lasts from December until March.

Rainfall varies greatly with elevation on Cyprus. About 15 inches of precipitation fall each year in the Mesaoria Plain, while the Troodos Mountains receive about 40 inches of rain and snow. Snow covers the higher elevations of the Troodos Mountains for up to two months of the year. In addition to severe summer droughts, Cyprus has experienced gradually decreasing rainfall over the past 30 years.

Heavy snow often falls in the upper elevations of the Troodos Mountains during the winter months (December to March).

Courtesy of Embassy of the Republic of Cyprus

13

Blooming trees and colorful spring flowers thrive in the mild, sunny climate of Cyprus.

High temperatures and drought limit the island's supply of drinking and irrigation water. The average summer temperature in Nicosia is 80° F, but temperatures can exceed 100° F in the capital during the season. Nicosia's temperatures average 50° F in December and only rarely fall to the freezing point. In the mountains, average temperatures are lower in both summer and winter.

Flora and Fauna

Despite heavy logging on Cyprus since ancient times, thick forests have survived on the slopes of the Troodos Mountains. Fires and armed conflict have further reduced the island's forests in the modern era. To protect the remaining trees, the government of southern Cyprus has created wooded reserves and has begun a reforestation program. Tree seedlings are also planted each year in northern Cyprus.

Coniferous (evergreen) trees flourish on the snow-clad slopes of Mount Olympus, the highest mountain in Cyprus. Beyond the foothills of Mount Olympus are the Morphou Plain and the Kyrenia Mountains of northern Cyprus.

The moufflon, a type of wild sheep, roams throughout remote wooded areas of the Troodos Mountains. Moufflons can climb higher than any hoofed animal except the mountain goat.

Nearly 20 percent of the island is now forested. Pine, cedar, and cypress trees are common on the slopes of the Troodos range. Oak, juniper, and olive trees also grow in Cyprus, and farmers have planted orchards of lemon, orange, and cherry trees. Hardy scrub vegetation replaces the mountain forests at lower elevations and on the Mesaoria Plain.

The moufflon, a mountain-dwelling sheep found only on Cyprus, still inhabits remote areas of the Troodos Mountains. Strict laws prevent hunting of this animal, whose numbers are decreasing. Many migrating birds spend part of the year in Cyprus, which lies along two important migratory routes. Flamingos winter in the salt lakes near Larnaca and Limassol. Snipes, quails, and partridges also inhabit the island.

Natural Resources

Extensive copper deposits on Cyprus made the island an important mining and trading center in ancient times. The Cypriots have not discovered additional copper reserves, however, and copper mining has nearly ceased. Asbestos and chromite

Winding dirt roads allow trucks to safely haul heavy equipment and other materials in and out of this mining site.

Nicosia, the capital and largest city on Cyprus, is a bustling cultural center. Although divided into Greek-speaking and Turkish-speaking areas by barbed-wire barriers, the city still attracts visitors with its unique architecture, museums, and markets.

have replaced copper as Cyprus's most important mineral resources.

Deposits of gypsum and marble provide important building materials. Road crews use sand and gravel from quarries (digging sites) for the construction of new highways. Both gypsum and bentonite (a clay with various manufacturing uses) remain significant mineral exports. Salt is extracted from the island's salt lakes. The woodlands on Cyprus supply part of the local demand for lumber.

Cities

About two-thirds of Cyprus's 700,000 people live in urban areas. Most of the island's large cities developed as trading ports along the seacoast. Armed conflict in the 1960s and 1970s forced many Greek-speaking refugees to flee from northern Cyprus to the ports of Limassol and Larnaca. Turkish Cypriots sought refuge in Kyrenia and in Morphou, a town on Morphou Bay. The capital of Nicosia was physically divided, and Famagusta in northern Cyprus lost much of its population and its position as the island's principal port. A small number of refugees from the Middle East have also arrived in the cities of southern Cyprus.

NICOSIA

Lying in the center of the Mesaoria Plain, Nicosia has been the capital of Cyprus since the twelfth century. The city was the scene of heavy fighting during the Turkish invasion of 1974. A barrier of barbed wire and fortified roadblocks now divides Nicosia into northern (Turkish-speaking) and southern (Greek-speaking) halves. About 75 percent of Nicosia's 160,000 people live in the Greek-speaking zone. Travel between the two areas is difficult for both residents and visitors.

Lefkon, the son of an Egyptian king, founded Nicosia in the fourth century B.C. After the fall of the Roman Empire in the fifth century A.D., marauding navies attacked the coast of Cyprus and drove many islanders to take refuge in this inland city. In the fifteenth century, Venetian princes from the Italian Peninsula made Nicosia their capital and built fortifications, castles, churches, and a protective wall. After Cyprus gained independence from Britain in 1960, Nicosia became the island republic's center of government.

Small industries in Nicosia make clothing, textiles, and shoes. Food-processing plants exist in the city's suburbs. The capital of both Greek- and Turkish-speaking regions of Cyprus, Nicosia has many government and administrative offices. Museums, palaces, churches, and mosques (Islamic houses of prayer) attract tourists despite the city's divided status.

Nicosia's original Venetian wall remains intact, and architecture from periods of Byzantine, Venetian, and British occupation still stands. One of the city's most famous landmarks is the thirteenth-century Cathedral of Santa Sophia. The Ottoman Turks transformed this Christian church into the Selimiye Mosque.

PORTS

The port of Limassol (population 120,000) lies on wide Akrotiri Bay in southern Cyprus. The island's second largest city, Limassol received many Greek-speaking refugees after the 1974 conflict. Other

A rapidly developing resort city situated on the southern coast, Limassol boasts a protected boat harbor and miles of sandy beaches.

refugees from Middle Eastern countries have also settled in the port. Nearby beaches have made Limassol a booming resort town, and new hotels and restaurants now line the coastal roads to the east and west of the city.

Limassol was a small settlement until a band of crusaders (Christian soldiers) made the site their headquarters in 1290. A towering crusader fortress, built to withstand attacks from both land and sea, still overlooks the busy harbor. Limassol has become the island's most important wine-producing and wine-exporting center, and numerous vineyards and wineries lie in the surrounding region.

Larnaca (population 35,000) is a port on the western end of Larnaca Bay, 40 miles northeast of Limassol. An international airport built just west of Larnaca has be-

come an important entry point for visitors to Cyprus. Cheese production and leather-making are Larnaca's major industries.

Mycenaeans from Greece first settled the area of modern Larnaca by 1200 B.C. Phoenicians—seagoing traders from the Middle East—arrived in the tenth century B.C. and settled in the ancient city of Kition, part of which lies within Larnaca. Wealth from sea trade transformed Kition into a powerful kingdom. During the rule of the Ottoman Turks—a time when many of the island's cities suffered an economic decline—Larnaca remained an important center of trade and shipping.

The largest city in Turkish-speaking northern Cyprus, Famagusta (population 41,000) was the island's most important port before 1974. In that year, civil conflict forced Famagusta's Greek-speaking

Courtesy of Embassy of the Republic of Cyprus

Tall palm trees line a busy thoroughfare in Larnaca.

A man bicycles toward a narrow gate that leads into the walled city of Famagusta, a port in northern Cyprus.

residents to flee south, and the port was closed. Forts built by the Venetians and the nearby ruins of Salamis, the island's largest ancient city, still attract some visitors to the area. The most important industry in Famagusta is the manufacture of footwear.

Ancient sites surround Paphos (population 12,000), which lies on the western coast of Cyprus. The ruins of Palea (old) Paphos, the original settlement, lie 10 miles to the southeast. The capital of Cyprus during the time of Roman occupation, Paphos became a small, poor village after the arrival of the crusaders. The dredging of the city's harbor in the early twentieth century increased commercial shipping and tourism. Although still a small town, Paphos is flourishing as a coastal resort center.

Pleasure boats anchor at a harbor in the coastal city of Paphos.

19

In ancient times, Salamis was the largest and wealthiest city on Cyprus. Once an independent kingdom, Salamis came under Roman rule in the first century B.C.

2) History and Government

Human settlement on Cyprus dates from about 6500 B.C. The first Cypriots were hunters and farmers who probably sailed to the island from Asia Minor or from the Middle East. Archaeologists have unearthed ancient stone weapons, tools, and the ruins of beehive-shaped dwellings at prehistoric sites in the Morphou Plain and in the short river valleys near the southern coast.

The early Cypriots built many of their towns near the seacoast and in the valleys of the Troodos Mountains. Later arrivals settled in the marshes and forested lowlands of the Morphou and Mesaoria plains. Farming and fishing remained the most important economic activities on Cyprus until the discovery of copper in the Troodos range.

The inhabitants of Cyprus began mining copper by 2000 B.C. They melted down the ore and combined it with other materials to make bronze, which metalworkers used to fashion strong weapons and tools. Cypriot merchants exported the finished bronze goods to the Middle East, to Asia Minor, and to Greece. Copper (*kypros* in Greek), from which the ancient Cypriots built a thriving trade, may even have given the island its name.

The ancient Cypriots also benefited from the island's fertile land and large stands of timber. Grains and fruits grew abundantly, and the Cypriots exported their timber to shipbuilding nations in the Mediterranean region. The islanders also exported pottery painted in a geometric style.

Ancient Cyprus had both valuable resources and a strategic location. Busy sea-lanes between Europe, the Middle East, and Africa lay near the island, making it a valuable prize for any leader who sought to control and profit from Mediterranean shipping.

Egyptian and Greek Settlement

The Cypriots traded many of their goods with Egypt, one of the most powerful ancient kingdoms in the Middle East. By about 1600 B.C., Egyptian merchants had established ports on the southern coast of Cyprus that later developed into the island's first large cities. Traders from the islands and from mainland cities of Greece also settled on Cyprus, bringing Greek culture and the Greek religion.

Around 1250 B.C., the kingdom of Mycenae in Greece was fighting the city of Troy in Asia Minor for control of islands and coastal cities in the Aegean Sea. Conflict was also brewing in the eastern Mediterranean. Middle Eastern peoples made devastating raids on Cyprus, causing the islanders to abandon mines, farms, and ports. Despite the raids, refugees from the conflicts in Greece and Asia Minor arrived on Cyprus, building new fortified settlements on the island's isolated bays. Many of these towns were destroyed, probably by earthquakes, during the eleventh century B.C.

The Greek settlers who survived on Cyprus then founded new settlements that eventually grew into powerful independent kingdoms. These Greek cities included Palea Paphos on the western coast, Salamis, and Kourion (west of Limassol). At this time, iron was replacing bronze as the basic raw material for weapons. The

This mosaic of a gladiator decorated the floor of a private home in the city of Kourion. In many ancient paintings and mosaics, names were placed above or below the figures to identify the gods, mythological characters, and royalty depicted by the artist.

skilled metalsmiths of Cyprus, who worked iron as well as bronze, exported their goods to Asia Minor, the Middle East, and Greece.

During the reigns of the ancient kings, ceramics, ironworking, and ivory carving became important industries in the busy Cypriot ports. Although much of mainland Greece fell into artistic and economic decline during this period, the ports of Cyprus continued to prosper from Mediterranean trade. The island's wealth and natural resources also attracted newcomers from both Greece and the Middle East.

Photo © Andrew E. Beswick

Masons and sculptors cut these underground burial chambers at Paphos directly from rock. The tombs housed the remains of Paphos's aristocratic Roman residents.

Middle Eastern Realms

In the mid-tenth century B.C., Phoenicians from the Middle East established new settlements on Cyprus. The largest of these was Kition, near modern Larnaca. Skilled sailors and merchants, the Phoenicians took over much of Cyprus's trade and exported Cypriot goods as far as Spain and Portugal in southwestern Europe.

The Phoenicians lived peacefully with the Greek-speaking Cypriots, but the island remained vulnerable to stronger realms that were conquering territory in the Middle East. In the late eighth century B.C., Assyria—a kingdom based in what is now Iraq—attacked both Phoenicia and Cyprus.

From 707 until 669 B.C., the Assyrian king forced the Greek and Phoenician rulers of Cyprus to pay a heavy tribute of money to spare the island from further attack. After the fall of Assyria in the sixth century B.C., Egypt occupied Cyprus for about 25 years.

Despite their forced payments to these realms, most large cities on Cyprus remained independent. Phoenician and

Independent Picture Service

During the reign of Sargon (above), king of Assyria, Cyprus was forced to pay tribute to the Assyrian Empire.

22

Evagoras *(center right)* captured the Phoenician city of Tyre and briefly united the towns of Cyprus under his rule. But the Greek leader fled Cyprus after the Persians defeated a naval force sent from Greece to help him.

Greek Cypriots continued competing for Cyprus's fertile land and profitable trade. When the powerful kingdom of Persia (modern Iran) invaded Cyprus around 550 B.C., the Phoenicians allied with the Persians to gain an advantage over the Greek Cypriots.

By 545 B.C., the Cypriots were paying tribute to the king of Persia. But Persian rule was harsh, and in 499 B.C. the Greek towns on Cyprus revolted. Although they received some help from mainland Greece and from Asia Minor, the Greek Cypriots were defeated. By 480 B.C., Phoenician leaders loyal to Persia had taken control of the island's largest towns. King Abdemon, who came to Cyprus from the Phoenician port of Tyre, banished Greek religion and Greek art from his kingdom in Salamis.

In the early fourth century B.C., Evagoras of Salamis, a Greek who had fled Abdemon's rule, returned from exile in Asia Minor and overthrew the Phoenician king. Evagoras made an alliance with Athens, a powerful Greek city. With the aid of the Athenians, Evagoras led a revolt in 391 B.C. that united the Greek Cypriot cities and temporarily ended Persian control. But the Persian navy defeated a force of Greek ships in 381 B.C., and Evagoras's death in 374 B.C. left the Greek Cypriots leaderless and disorganized. Within a few years, Cyprus was again under Persian domination.

The Ptolemaic Kings

While Cyprus remained a Persian possession, the leaders of the growing kingdom

Photo by Bettmann Archive

Ptolemy I became the king of Egypt after the death of Alexander the Great. Ptolemy's successors in Egypt – known as the Ptolemaic kings – brought Cyprus into their realm.

of Macedonia, in northern Greece, were challenging Persian rule in Asia Minor. Alexander the Great, a brilliant Macedonian commander, fought and defeated the Persians in Phoenicia and captured Tyre in 332 B.C. The Greek Cypriots sent soldiers, horses, and ships to help Alexander in his campaign. As a result of their defeat in Phoenicia, the Persians abandoned Cyprus. Alexander then brought the island under his control.

After Alexander's death in 323 B.C., his realm passed to several of his officers. Cyprus became a possession of Ptolemy I, a Macedonian general who had established a new dynasty (ruling family) in Egypt. His successors—known as the Ptolemaic kings—took direct control of the kingdoms on Cyprus.

Under the Ptolemaic dynasty, the city of Nea (new) Paphos replaced Salamis as the island's administrative center. Nea Paphos

lay on the western coast of Cyprus not far from a famous temple dedicated to the Greek goddess Aphrodite. As religious pilgrims and Greek merchants arrived in Nea Paphos, the city grew as a center of Greek culture and religion in the eastern Mediterranean.

Cyprus experienced peace and prosperity under the Ptolemaic kings. Although the Cypriot cities had lost their independence, the island's timber and mineral resources continued to bring wealth to its inhabitants. At the same time, however, the growing republic of Rome on the Italian Peninsula was expanding its control in southern Europe. Cyprus attracted the attention of Roman leaders who sought to establish a strategic outpost in the eastern Mediterranean.

When pirates captured a Roman official off the coast of Cyprus in 67 B.C., Ptolemaios—the island's king—agreed to pay only a small amount for ransom. Considering this action an insult, the official returned to Rome and passed a law that made Cyprus a Roman province. In 58 B.C., when Roman armies arrived to take possession of the island, Ptolemaios committed suicide.

Roman Rule and Christianity

After their conquest of Cyprus, the Romans made the island part of the Roman province of Syria, a territory in the Middle East. Several times over the next few decades, however, Rome and the Ptolemaic leaders of Egypt exchanged possession of the island. By 22 B.C., Cyprus was again part of the Roman Empire, and a Roman proconsul (governor) was ruling from Nea Paphos.

In the next century, a new religion, Christianity, arose in the Middle East. A Christian leader, the apostle Paul, arrived on Cyprus in A.D. 45 to gain converts to the new faith. Paul was accompanied by Barnabas, a citizen of Salamis. Although the Romans executed Barnabas for his beliefs, Paul converted the proconsul of Nea Paphos to Christianity. Soon Christians were building churches and monasteries at many sites on Cyprus, which became the first territory in the world to be governed by a Christian.

Roman rule continued on Cyprus for several hundred years after the arrival of Christianity. Sea trade, metalworking, and agriculture supported the island's growing population. Wealthy Roman officials built theaters, villas, public buildings, and stadiums at Nea Paphos, Salamis, Kourion,

and many other coastal cities. The empire's strong navy and land forces assured peace and stability in the Mediterranean region.

By the late fourth century A.D., however, Rome was losing territory along its frontiers in northern Europe. Rebellion against Roman rule erupted in the Middle East, and piracy in the Mediterranean disrupted trade. Many cities on Cyprus were in decline when severe earthquakes in 332 and 342 destroyed much of Nea Paphos and Salamis. Although the islanders restored

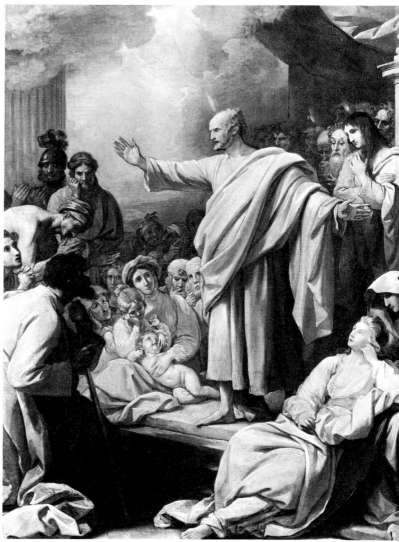

The apostle Paul preached the new faith of Christianity in the first century A.D. Paul converted the Roman governor of Cyprus to Christian beliefs, and Christians later built many churches on the island.

25

their religious and public buildings, none of the large Cypriot ports regained their former wealth.

Internal rivalries were also weakening the Roman Empire. By 395 the realm split into eastern and western halves. The old imperial capital of Rome still controlled the Western Empire, which included territory in western Europe. Cyprus became a part of the Eastern, or Byzantine, Empire. The leaders of the Byzantine Empire made the Greek city of Constantinople (modern Istanbul) their capital.

Byzantine Cyprus

Cyprus remained a Byzantine possession after the fall of the Western Empire in the mid-fifth century. The island was directly controlled by the Byzantine governor of Antioch, a city in Syria. The Cypriots, however, sought an end to outside control of their island. The actions of Cyprus's religious leaders later helped to bring about a degree of self-rule for the Cypriots.

In 488 Anthemios, the Christian archbishop of Cyprus, discovered the tomb of Barnabas, the companion of the apostle Paul. Anthemios brought relics from the tomb to Zeno, the Byzantine emperor. Impressed by the finds, Zeno granted the Christian leaders on Cyprus the freedom to direct religious services and to run much of the island's civil government. This action lessened the authority of Byzantine administrators on Cyprus.

Photo by SCALA/Art Resource

The emperor Justinian (center, with bowl) **brought new territories into his realm, including Cyprus, which offered safe harbors for Byzantine ships in the Mediterranean.**

In the sixth century, much of the Byzantine Empire experienced civil unrest and invasion. Cyprus remained peaceful, however, and Byzantine forces used the island as a base for expeditions to the Middle East and Africa. In addition, as trade in the eastern Mediterranean became an important part of the Byzantine economy, the busy ports of Cyprus regained some of their former wealth.

THE ARAB CONQUEST

The breakup of the Roman Empire had brought about chaos in the Middle East, where many different peoples were claiming territory. The leaders of Islam, a new religion, began spreading their faith in the region in the early seventh century. Muslims (followers of Islam) formed powerful armies to conquer and convert peoples of the Middle East and North Africa. In 647 a force of Saracens, an Islamic people from the Arabian Peninsula, invaded Cyprus. Muslim armies eventually threw off Byzantine control and brought the island under the authority of the Islamic caliph (ruler) of Damascus in Syria.

Over the next three centuries, Cyprus suffered further raids by Arabs and counterattacks by Byzantine forces. Both sides plundered coastal cities, forcing thousands of Cypriots into captivity or exile. The island changed hands several times until 965, when the Byzantine emperor Nicephoros Phocas recaptured Cyprus.

After the Byzantine reconquest, the islanders founded the port cities of Limassol, Larnaca, and Famagusta. The *katapan,* or Byzantine governor, directed the building of new Christian churches in Nicosia. In the eleventh century, disagreements between Christian religious leaders in Rome and Constantinople led to the division of the Roman Catholic Church into Western (or Latin) and Eastern Orthodox sects. Cyprus's location close to the birthplace of Christianity made it an important outpost of the Eastern Orthodox Church.

Photo by Drs. A. A. M. van der Heyden, Naarden, the Netherlands

This mosque (Islamic place of prayer) was built in the Syrian city of Damascus during the reign of the Umayyad dynasty (family of rulers). The Umayyads introduced the Islamic religion to the Mediterranean region and conquered Cyprus in the seventh century A.D.

Photo © Andrew E. Beswick

Kolossi Castle was built on Cyprus by crusaders (religious warriors) from western Europe. The crusaders made Cyprus a base for their campaign to recapture holy sites in the Middle East.

27

The Lusignan Kings

In the 1100s and 1200s, Christian knights from western Europe—known as crusaders—arrived to conquer territory in the Middle East. The knights and their armies battled Islamic forces for control of the region's holy sites, including the city of Jerusalem (now in Israel). In the twelfth century, the crusaders set up a new kingdom at Jerusalem, which was a holy site for both Muslims and Christians. The English king and crusader Richard the Lion-Hearted conquered Cyprus in 1191. In the following year, Richard left Cyprus to carry on his crusade in the Middle East.

He made an agreement to turn Cyprus over to a French nobleman, Guy de Lusignan, who had lost the throne of Jerusalem to Richard's nephew. Guy arrived in 1192 to take possession of Cyprus.

Guy was the first of the Lusignan dynasty, which ruled Cyprus for several centuries. The Lusignans—who were members of the Latin (Roman Catholic) sect—built strong fortifications in the Kyrenia Mountains. To avoid attacks along the island's coast, they made the inland city of Nicosia their capital. The kings who took up residence in Nicosia raised splendid palaces and Catholic cathedrals. The

Courtesy of Wayland Picture Library

The English king and crusader Richard the Lion-Hearted (left) captured Cyprus in 1191 but left the island in the next year to fight in the Middle East.

Lusignans also made the Roman Catholic Church the official Cypriot church. In 1220 a Roman Catholic leader replaced the Eastern Orthodox archbishop of Cyprus.

Many crusaders later sought refuge on Cyprus after suffering defeats in the Middle East. The crusaders seized farmland from Cypriot peasants and took possession of large estates created by the Lusignans. A new system of landownership known as feudalism was brought to Cyprus by the crusaders, who had known this system in western Europe. Under the feudal system, farmers who worked and lived on the land had to turn over a percentage of their crops each year to the landowners.

The Crusades ended in failure when Jerusalem fell to Muslim armies in 1291. Nevertheless, trade between Cyprus and the Middle East continued. Taxes and duties on the goods passing through the island's ports made the Lusignan kings rich enough to form new armies. Peter I, a Lusignan of the mid-fourteenth century, carried out successful raids on Islamic territory in both Asia Minor and Egypt during his reign.

Photo by Bettmann Archive

In 1472 the Venetian noblewoman Caterina Cornaro married James II, the king of Cyprus. She succeeded her husband after his death in the next year but returned to Venice in 1489.

VENICE AND GENOA

By the time of Peter I's reign, Cyprus was thriving. Many different peoples and cultures existed side by side in the island's ports. Yet these harbors lacked natural defenses and remained vulnerable to attack and conquest. Genoa and Venice, wealthy states on the Italian Peninsula, fought over Famagusta, which had become the busiest port on Cyprus. Genoan forces took Famagusta from the Lusignans in the 1370s, and in the next century the Egyptian navy attacked Limassol and Larnaca. To avoid further invasion, the Lusignans eventually agreed to pay tribute to the Egyptians.

The ties between Cyprus and Venice strengthened during the 1400s. The last Lusignan king of Cyprus, James II, married Caterina Cornaro, a member of a wealthy and powerful Venetian family. James died under mysterious circumstances in 1473, and his infant son died the next year. In 1489 Caterina Cornaro gave up the throne of Cyprus and turned the island over to Venice.

The Ottoman Conquest

The Venetians used Cyprus as a base for their huge merchant fleet in the Mediterranean. But the Ottoman Turks of Asia Minor were challenging the Venetians. In 1453 the Ottomans had attacked and conquered Constantinople, causing the fall of the Byzantine Empire. Eventually, Greece, Egypt, and much of the Middle East also came under Ottoman control. In 1570 the Turks invaded Cyprus from Asia Minor. Nicosia and Famagusta fell within a year, and in 1573 Venice gave up all its claims to Cyprus.

The Turks ended the feudal system on Cyprus and allowed the island's peasants to own small plots of land. But the new rulers also collected heavy taxes from the inhabitants, which eventually harmed agriculture and trade. Famine killed many Cypriots and drought turned much of the island's productive soil into infertile wasteland.

After conquering Cyprus, the Turks— who were Muslims—allowed officials of the Eastern Orthodox Church to return. Throughout the period of Ottoman rule, the Orthodox faith gave the Greek-speaking inhabitants of Cyprus a common religion and culture. All Roman Catholic churches, however, were transformed into mosques. In addition, many Turkish soldiers and their families moved from Asia Minor to Cyprus. This settlement of new farms and villages created two separate Cypriot communities —Greek-speakers and Turkish-speakers.

In the mid-1700s, the Turkish sultan (ruler) turned over the administration of the Greek-speaking regions of the island to the Eastern Orthodox archbishop of Cyprus. By this arrangement, the sultan ruled Cy-

Courtesy of Cultural and Tourism Office of the Turkish Embassy

The Ottoman Turks defeated the Venetian forces on Cyprus in the 1570s and brought the island into their growing Islamic empire. Under Ottoman rule, many settlers from Asia Minor (mainland Turkey) arrived on Cyprus, creating a new society of Turkish-speaking Cypriots.

The mosque of Arap Ahmet, in what is now the northern (Turkish-speaking) section of Nicosia, dates to the early nineteenth century. While the Ottoman Empire ruled Cyprus, both Eastern Orthodox and Islamic places of worship remained open.

Photo by M. Ergün Olgun

prus indirectly and maintained the island as a military base. Orthodox officials were responsible for collecting taxes from the Greek Cypriots and for turning the money over to the sultan's representative.

At the same time, resistance to Ottoman rule was growing in Greece. Greek merchants who operated in the Mediterranean supported this rebellion, which quickly spread to Cyprus. By 1821 an armed revolt had broken out in many areas of Greece. Several western European states sent aid to the Greek rebels to weaken Ottoman power in the eastern Mediterranean.

The Turks eventually recognized an independent Greek republic, but the sultan was determined to hold on to Cyprus. During the rebellion, he ordered the execution of the Cypriot archbishop and of several other Greek Cypriot leaders. Although a large portion of Greece gained independence by the 1830s, on Cyprus the Ottoman Empire remained firmly in control.

Mediterranean Conflicts

Throughout the 1800s, the Ottoman Empire suffered a steady decline in its military and economic power. Other states and leaders in the region saw this as a chance to gain territory at the sultan's expense. At the same time, Cyprus became a target for European nations—including Britain and Russia—that were trying to control strategic ports and trade in the Mediterranean.

In the 1830s, Muhammad Ali Pasha, the Ottoman governor of Egypt, rebelled against the sultan by attacking Turkish forces in the Middle East. To extend its power in the region, Russia allied itself with Muhammad Ali. But Britain, not wanting Russia or Egypt to occupy Cyprus, allied with Turkey and stopped Muhammad Ali's forces from overthrowing the Ottoman Empire. Britain then demanded that the sultan make reforms in the administration of Cyprus.

British officers raised their country's flag on Cyprus in 1878.

Photo by Bettmann Archive

BRITISH ADMINISTRATION

The conflict between Turkey and Russia continued through the middle of the nineteenth century. War erupted in 1877, and by the next year Russia had gained the upper hand. Turkey, hoping to prevent a Russian invasion of Cyprus, allowed Britain to take over the island's administration. In return Britain agreed to use a portion of its revenue from Cyprus to pay Turkey's debts. The Greek Cypriots, who were opposed to British control, demanded political union with Greece. The British officials who governed the island refused this demand.

Under British administration, the economic and living conditions on Cyprus gradually improved. The British put their own legal and educational systems into place and built new roads and bridges on the island. Agricultural production and foreign trade increased. Turkish-speakers —who had been settling on Cyprus since the late sixteenth century—remained on the island.

The World Wars

At the start of the twentieth century, Cyprus was a quiet British protectorate. Legally the island was still part of the Ottoman Empire, but the sultan had little control over either Greek- or Turkish-speaking Cypriots. Greeks and Turks lived side by side in many Cypriot towns and villages, and both Islamic mosques and Orthodox churches remained open. Greek- and Turkish-language schools educated the children of the two communities. Although the island's Greek population was

32

growing restless with foreign rule, there was little violence.

Events in Europe, however, were moving many nations toward war. Britain eventually allied with France, Russia, and other countries to oppose Germany. When the conflict known as World War I broke out in 1914, Turkey joined the German side. Although Greece had often fought against the Ottoman Empire before 1914, its government remained neutral at the start of the war. Britain offered to turn Cyprus over to Greece in return for a military alliance, but the Greek government refused. Soon thereafter, Britain annexed the island from Turkey.

After four years of bloody ground combat in Europe, Germany surrendered in the fall of 1918. By the Treaty of Lausanne, which was signed after the war, Turkey permanently lost its claim to Cyprus. In 1925 the island became a British crown colony—a direct possession of the British monarch.

During the 1920s and 1930s, Greek Cypriots made frequent demands for a union of Cyprus with Greece. After violent demonstrations erupted in 1931, the British governor imposed a state of emergency. The British banned all demonstrations and political activity on Cyprus for the next 10 years.

In Europe, meanwhile, Germany and its ally Italy were again becoming a serious military threat. After Germany invaded Poland in the summer of 1939, World War II broke out. Britain and its allies were soon fighting German and Italian forces in the Mediterranean region. Germany invaded Greece in 1941 and occupied the country for four years. After the war ended in 1945, conflict between political factions caused famine, poverty, and violence in Greece.

POSTWAR CONFLICTS

Although the British offered a new constitution to the people of Cyprus after the war, a majority of the Greek Cypriots rejected the document in a referendum (public vote). In 1950 the Greek Orthodox Church of Cyprus organized another referendum on *enosis*, the Greek word for union. After the voting, the church claimed that 96 percent of the islanders had cast their ballots for union with Greece.

Nevertheless, British leaders felt that the island's strategic position—as well as Greece's fragile government and economy—made Cypriot independence or enosis unwise. In addition, the Turkish government opposed self-rule for Cyprus, because it might bring about enosis against the will of the Turkish Cypriots. The Turks contended that the island should be divided into independent Greek- and Turkish-speaking areas.

Courtesy of Embassy of the Republic of Cyprus

Archbishop Makarios, a popular Greek Cypriot religious leader, became president of Cyprus after the island gained its independence from Britain in 1960. Although he favored the union *(enosis)* of Cyprus and Greece in the 1950s, Makarios later changed his position.

In the mid-1950s, the situation gradually grew violent. Guerrilla groups made up of pro-enosis Greek Cypriots sabotaged British military installations and attacked British personnel. With the support of the Greek government, Archbishop Makarios, the leader of the Eastern Orthodox Church on Cyprus, demanded self-rule. In response, the British forced the Greek Cypriot leader into exile. This action led to increased violence that finally prompted the United Nations (UN), an international diplomatic organization, to call for negotiations.

Although ready to allow some form of self-rule on Cyprus, British leaders realized that cooperation among the Cypriots, and between Greece and Turkey, were the keys to the island's future. But all attempts by the Greek and Turkish governments to resolve their differences over Cyprus failed. In addition, Britain's own interest in keeping its military bases on the island complicated the situation.

Independence

In 1958 diplomats from Greece and Turkey met with Greek and Turkish Cypriots in Zurich, Switzerland. The parties agreed on the form of government for an independent Cyprus. Later in the year, representatives of Britain, Greece, and Turkey signed the agreement. Cyprus officially became the independent Republic of Cyprus on August 16, 1960.

The new government had a specified number of Greek- and Turkish-speaking officials. Greek Cypriots voted for the president, while Turkish Cypriots elected the vice president. Either leader could veto legislation passed by Cyprus's House of Representatives. The Zurich treaty banned any division of the island and forbade union with any foreign nation. Britain, Greece, and Turkey reserved the right to intervene if the provisions of the treaty were broken. In 1961 another agreement allowed Britain to maintain control of its two military bases on Cyprus.

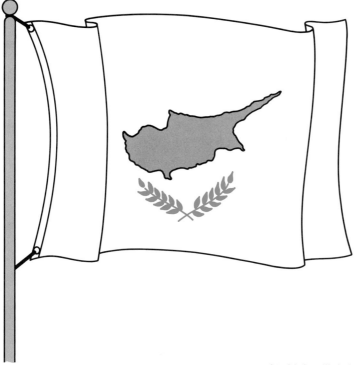

The flag of Cyprus was adopted by the republic's government after independence. The color yellow represents the island's copper deposits, and two olive branches stand for the hope for peace between Greek and Turkish Cypriots. The flag's designer avoided the use of either Greek or Turkish national colors or political symbols.

Artwork by Laura Westlund

The House of Representatives, the legislature of the Republic of Cyprus, meets in Nicosia. Turkish delegates withdrew from this chamber in 1963 and later formed a separate administration for the northern part of Cyprus.

The new leaders of Cyprus were Archbishop Makarios—who returned from exile to become the first president of independent Cyprus—and Fazil Kuchuk, the Turkish vice president. The two men frequently disagreed on constitutional matters, however, and the republic's complicated system of representation quickly became unworkable. In December 1963, after Makarios proposed changes to the constitution, the Turkish Cypriots withdrew from their posts. The government, left in the hands of Greek Cypriots, now had little authority over the Turkish-speakers living on the island.

CIVIL CONFLICT

By 1964 Cyprus had again become the scene of violent clashes between Greek- and Turkish-speakers. The UN and Britain sent forces to the island to curb the fighting, and the UN put a cease-fire into effect in August 1964. But tensions on Cyprus remained high. Most Turkish Cypriots, who had no representation in the republic's government, favored the

Within Nicosia, a barrier of barbed wire and fences still divides the Greek Cypriot and Turkish Cypriot neighborhoods.

The village of Yerolakos suffered severe damage during the invasion of northern Cyprus in the summer of 1974.

division of Cyprus to protect their rights. A committee led by a British diplomat drew up a "Green Line" in Nicosia that divided the capital's Greek and Turkish neighborhoods.

Archbishop Makarios won presidential elections in 1968 and 1973. Many Greek Cypriots were still calling for union with Greece, although Makarios had changed his position and now opposed enosis. During this time, continuing violence was forcing many Turkish Cypriots to flee to villages in northern Cyprus. These settlements became semi-independent areas with their own Turkish leaders and militias. In 1967 Turkish Cypriots set up a provisional government to administer Turkish areas in northern Cyprus.

WAR AND DIVISION

In the late 1960s, a group of Greek army officers overthrew their elected government and formed a junta (ruling committee) in Greece. In July 1974, the members of the junta supported the overthrow of

Makarios by pro-enosis Greek Cypriots. After Makarios fled the island, he was replaced by Nikos Sampson, a newspaper publisher who strongly favored union with Greece.

Fearing that Sampson would declare the island a part of Greece, Turkey invaded northern Cyprus on July 20 with a force of tanks, artillery, and troops. A cease-fire two days later brought about the collapse of Sampson's government. Despite the cease-fire and the presence of British and UN troops, violence and widespread destruction continued on Cyprus until late August. By then, the Turkish army had occupied the northern one-third of the island.

The UN forces set up a series of roadblocks, barricades, and barbed-wire fences along the Attila Line, a new barrier between northern and southern Cyprus. The Attila Line ran west from Kato Pyrgos, on Morphou Bay, through Nicosia and to the east coast just south of Famagusta. As a result of the fighting, about 200,000 Greek

Cypriots fled to southern Cyprus, and about 50,000 Turkish Cypriots fled to the north. In 1975 the inhabitants of Turkish-occupied Cyprus declared their portion of the island a self-governing region.

Recent Events

Makarios, who remained a hero to the Greek Cypriots, returned to Cyprus and in December 1974 again became president of the republic. After Makarios died in 1977, Spyros Kyprianou assumed the presidency. The Greek Cypriot voters reelected Kyprianou in 1978 and 1983. During this time, attempts by the UN to initiate talks to resolve the island's political division ended in failure. Although various agreements were signed by the two Cypriot communities in the late 1970s, they were not put into effect.

On November 15, 1983, Turkish Cypriots declared the establishment of the Turkish Republic of Northern Cyprus. Only Turkey recognized this state, which has no representation in the UN. The Turkish Cypriots

Courtesy of Embassy of the Republic of Cyprus

George Vassiliou won a five-year term as president of the Republic of Cyprus in 1988.

Courtesy of U.N. High Commissioner for Refugees/Jean Mohr

In 1974 three Greek Cypriot children strolled through a refugee camp set up after fighting broke out on Cyprus between Greek Cypriot and Turkish forces. Although the refugees have been resettled, some Greek and Turkish Cypriots still have claims on property that was lost during the conflict.

Raouf Denktash, president of the Republic of Northern Cyprus, has been a leading representative of the Turkish Cypriots since the 1960s.

formed their own government, consisting of a president and a prime minister as chief executives and a national assembly of elected representatives.

Negotiations continued throughout the 1980s, but Turkish and Greek Cypriots made no progress toward reunification. In the summer of 1991, the United States attempted to organize an international conference that would include Raouf Denktash, the Turkish Cypriot leader, and George Vassiliou, who was elected president of the Republic of Cyprus in 1988.

Although Greek and Turkish Cypriots agree on a future federation of two semi-independent regions, the two sides cannot agree on the republic's constitution. Greeks favor a strong central government, while Turks want a much looser association. The two sides also disagree on the future of Cypriot refugees, many of whom wish to return to their homes on either side of the Attila Line. The reunification of Cy-

prus would improve economic conditions on the island, but Greek and Turkish Cypriots, as well as the governments of Greece and Turkey, are making little progress toward that goal.

Government

Established in 1960, the government of the Republic of Cyprus maintains authority over the southern two-thirds of the divided island. Every five years, adult voters over the age of 21 elect the republic's president, who can veto laws passed by the legislature. The president appoints an 11-member Council of Ministers to run the government's various departments. Voters also elect the 50 members of the House of Representatives, the republic's unicameral (one-house) legislature. The legislature's 24 Turkish representatives withdrew from the chamber in 1963.

The Turkish Republic of Northern Cyprus has a similar form of government. Voters 18 years of age and older elect the president, but the prime minister in northern Cyprus acts as the chief executive. The 50-member assembly can vote to elect or replace the prime minister.

Cyprus is divided into six districts, each of which is headed by a district officer who represents the central governments. Two of these districts, Kyrenia and Famagusta, lie within northern Cyprus. Municipal councils run cities and towns, while village commissions are elected to administer smaller settlements.

Separate judicial systems hold authority in northern and southern Cyprus. In both regions, assize and district courts hear cases in each administrative district. Assize courts have authority over all criminal cases. District courts hear property, civil, and criminal cases. Cases can be appealed to the supreme courts, which also decide matters of constitutional and legislative law. In southern Cyprus, a system of Eastern Orthodox courts has authority over religious cases.

Using a chisel and mallet, a woodcarver creates an intricately designed altar for a church in Nicosia.

3) The People

The social divisions on the island of Cyprus closely follow the physical division that occurred in 1974. Of the 700,000 inhabitants of Cyprus, about 77 percent are of Greek heritage. Almost all of these Greek Cypriots live south of the Attila Line. Northern Cyprus is home to most of the Turkish Cypriots, who make up 22 percent of the island's total population. Since 1974 about 65,000 of these Turkish Cypriots have come from Asia Minor to settle in the area. The remaining 1 percent of the island's inhabitants are Muslim and Chris-tian refugees of Middle Eastern conflicts. Many of these immigrants arrived from Lebanon and live in the ports of southern Cyprus.

The 1974 conflict forced Greek Cypriots in the north and Turkish Cypriots in the south to abandon their property and flee across the Attila Line. Although many refugees expect to return to their former homes, most have settled into new communities. In addition, strict military control along the Attila Line prevents Cypriots from traveling between northern and southern Cyprus. The island's Greek and Turkish administrations have been unable to agree on the future status of these refugees or on their property claims.

About two-thirds of the people of Cyprus live in cities and towns along the island's coasts. The fertile Mesaoria and Morphou plains have a high concentration of people who make their living from agriculture. Only small towns and villages exist in the Troodos and Kyrenia mountains. The overall population density of Cyprus is 196 persons per square mile. Population growth, once rapid on the island, has slowed to 1 percent—a low rate among countries in the eastern Mediterranean region. At that rate, the island's population will take 71 years to double.

Religion and Festivals

Nearly all Greek Cypriots belong to the Church of Cyprus, an independent branch of the Eastern Orthodox Church. During the island's turbulent history, church officials served as both religious and political leaders for Greek Cypriots seeking independence from foreign rule. Orthodox clergy still preside at baptisms, weddings, and holiday services for the majority of Greek Cypriots.

The primate (leader) of the Church of Cyprus is also the bishop of Nicosia. Church members elect the primate and the island's three other Orthodox bishops. Many monasteries—independent religious communities—still exist in remote areas of the coast and in the Troodos Mountains. Maronite Christians, members of a Christian sect that began in Lebanon, and Roman Catholics also live in southern Cyprus.

Easter—celebrated with feasts, religious services, and parades—is the most important religious holiday for Orthodox Christians. Greek Cypriots observe Independence Day on October 1, and Ochi ("No") Day, a celebration of Greek resistance to an invasion by Italian forces during World War II, on October 28.

Courtesy of Embassy of the Republic of Cyprus

Monks of the Apostle Barnabas Monastery work on an icon—a detailed religious painting. Eastern Orthodox believers, who consider the paintings sacred, display icons in homes and churches and carry them in religious processions.

Turkish-speakers follow the Islamic faith, which was brought to Cyprus by the Ottoman Turks in the late sixteenth century. Islam centers on the will of God (Allah) as revealed to the prophet Muhammad in the Koran, the Muslim holy book. Devout Muslims pray five times a day and make a pilgrimage to the Islamic holy city of Mecca in Saudi Arabia if they are able. A *mufti,* or Islamic religious leader, directs the Islamic church on Cyprus.

The Ottoman Turks converted many Roman Catholic cathedrals into Islamic mosques. One of the largest mosques in northern Cyprus is Nicosia's Selimiye Mosque, which was originally the medieval Cathedral of Santa Sophia.

Turkish Cypriots observe Victory Day, a celebration of the Turkish defeat of Greek forces after World War I, on August 30. On November 15, Turkish Cypriots mark the establishment of the Turkish Republic of Northern Cyprus. Religious holidays for Muslim Cypriots include the birthday of Muhammad on January 8. During the month of Ramadan, Muslims observe a fast, taking neither food or drink between sunrise and sunset.

Health and Education

Cypriots enjoy a generally high level of health and educational services. A mild climate and a lack of polluting industries contribute to the island's health standards. Government vaccination programs have eliminated once-common local diseases, including malaria. The leading causes of death in the early 1990s were heart disease, cancer, and car accidents.

Life expectancy on Cyprus is 76 years. Infant mortality—the number of babies who die within one year of birth—is 11 per 1,000. These rates are average for Mediterranean countries but better than figures for countries in the Middle East.

Public health services provide care for people living in rural areas and in small towns in southern and northern Cyprus. A system of clinics, hospitals, and pharmacies operates throughout the island. Private, employer-sponsored health programs

Photo © Andrew E. Beswick

A social-security program and good pension benefits allow Cyprus's elderly citizens to enjoy a comfortable standard of living.

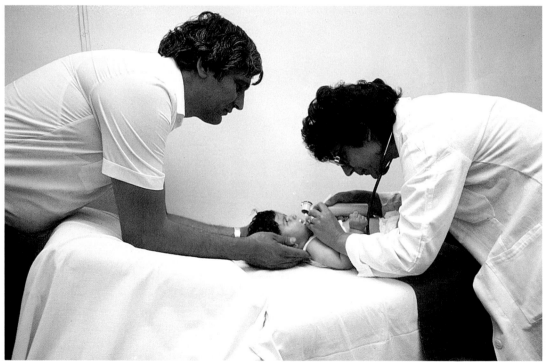

World Bank Photo

A health-care worker examines a small child in a rural clinic. City hospitals and village clinics provide medical care for people living on Cyprus.

Assisted by their teacher, kindergarten students assemble puzzles and create small-scale buildings with wooden blocks. Primary-school students are taught basic reading, writing, and math skills. Instructors also give special emphasis to art, music, language, and environmental subjects.

cover most urban workers. A social-security system supports health services and pensions for retired and disabled workers.

Primary schooling on Cyprus is free and compulsory. The government has built elementary schools in every town with more than 15 students. Area schools serve smaller communities. After six years of primary schooling, students in southern Cyprus attend two three-year secondary schools—the *lyceum* and the *gymnasium* —that are patterned on the Greek system. The gymnasium instructs 12- through 14-year-olds in basic subjects such as history and geography. The lyceum, for students 15 through 17 years of age, offers either elective subjects or a vocational course of study. In northern Cyprus, students attend a six-year secondary school after their elementary education.

Private institutions, including foreign schools and religious academies, also exist on Cyprus. Many children and adults attend private, part-time foreign-language schools in the island's larger cities. There are postsecondary schools of teacher training, nursing, and hotel management. The University of Cyprus was established in 1989 and began operating in 1992. Cyprus also has the leading forestry college in the Middle East. Many Cypriot students pursue postsecondary degrees at four-year colleges in Europe and in the United States.

The restored Roman theater at the ancient city of Kourion seats a 3,500-member audience for its open-air performances.

Language and Literature

Greek and Turkish are the dominant languages on Cyprus. Greek, an Indo-European tongue, arrived with the first Greek settlers during the Mycenaean period. After the fall of the Western Roman Empire in the fifth century A.D., Greek remained the language of the Byzantine Empire and of the Eastern Orthodox Church. Scholars believe that the Greek dialect spoken on Cyprus is close to ancient Greek.

Turkish, one of the Ural-Altaic languages that originated in central Asia, is used in media, schools, and government in northern Cyprus. English is also widely spoken on the island, and private language schools that specialize in English have made many Cypriots bilingual (able to speak two languages). Greek and Turkish newspapers circulate in the two communities, and English-language papers are on sale throughout the island.

Literature on Cyprus began with the epic poetry sung by bards (singing poets) at the wealthy ancient port of Salamis. Stasinos, an ancient Greek inhabitant of Cyprus, wrote the epic poem *Kypria,* which told legends of the island's early history. Poets and musicians staged festivals in the temples at Paphos and Kition.

Isokrates, a Greek teacher who arrived on Cyprus in the fourth century B.C., wrote an account of the invasion and harsh rule

Photo by Bettmann Archive

Born on Cyprus, the Greek philosopher Zeno founded the Stoic school of philosophy, which flourished from about 300 B.C. to A.D. 300. Stoicism, which honors reason over emotion, greatly influenced law, ethics, and political theory in the Mediterranean region.

of the ancient Persians. Zeno, one of the most famous ancient Greek philosophers, was born on Cyprus. After moving to Athens, Zeno founded the Stoic school of philosophy, which held that people should face life without emotion and according to reason.

Italian and French literary forms influenced Cypriot authors under the Lusignan kings. Leontias Machairas wrote *The Tale of the Sweet Land of Cyprus* in the early fifteenth century. Unlike many histories of the time, this work was written in prose and not in verse. Love poetry composed in the Cypriot dialect in the 1500s imitated famous Italian writers, especially the poet Petrarch.

During the Ottoman period, many popular Turkish poets *(meddah)* thrived in Cyprus. The contemporary Turkish Cypriot poet Osman Turkay has won many international awards and is known for his futuristic themes.

Modern poetry in demotic (conversational) Greek remains an important literary form in both Greece and Cyprus. Loukis Acritas (1909–1965) wrote plays and novels about Greek and Cypriot society and history. Greek Cypriots also enjoy the works of the ancient Greek playwrights, including Sophocles and Euripides. Theater companies stage Greek and Shakespearean plays at the restored ancient theaters of Salamis, Kourion, and Soloi.

The Arts

The extensive archaeological remains on Cyprus are the island's most important artistic legacy. The wealthy ancient kingdoms of Cyprus built numerous temples dedicated to the Greek and Roman gods. Skilled Greek sculptors carved beautiful statues of the goddess Aphrodite for the ancient port of Paphos. Artists decorated the House of Dionysus, the home of a Roman official in Paphos, with elaborate floor mosaics made of brightly colored stones. Early Christian churches, patterned closely after Roman temples, have also survived near the ancient cities.

Christianity and Byzantine rule brought new subjects and styles to artists working

Photo © Andrew E. Beswick

Ancient Greeks and Romans set brightly colored stones in mortar to create ornate patterns. This mosaic was **uncovered** at the ruins of Soloi in northwestern Cyprus.

These arches, which were built while Cyprus was under Byzantine rule, stand amid Roman ruins near Paphos. Archaeologists have unearthed architecturally important sites throughout the island.

Photo © Andrew E. Beswick

on Cyprus. Orthodox believers placed icons, or paintings on wooden panels, on church altars as well as in private homes. Colorful mosaics and frescoes also decorated Byzantine churches and monasteries. The Lusignan kings raised elaborate cathedrals and palaces in the French Gothic style. The Ottoman Turks brought the Islamic religion and converted many Catholic cathedrals into mosques. The Hala Sultan Tekke, a Muslim shrine west of Larnaca in southern Cyprus, shelters the remains of Umm Haram, the aunt of Muhammad.

Photo © Andrew E. Beswick

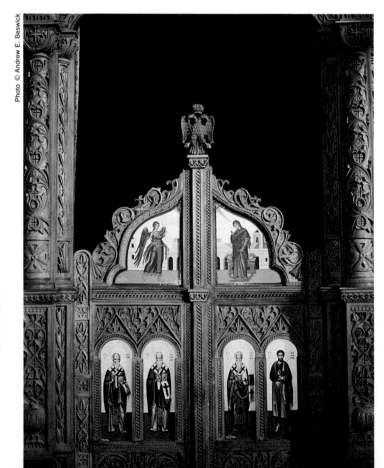

Artisans use icons and wooden carvings to decorate Eastern Orthodox churches. Large panels—called iconostases—often act as screens between the sanctuary and the congregation.

46

A woman forms a water jug with the help of a manually operated wheel. Cypriots have made and used ceramic pottery for thousands of years.

The style of many modern buildings on Cyprus owes much to the island's artistic past. Architects who created the elaborate Archbishop's Palace in Nicosia, completed in 1956, used Venetian designs on the exterior of the building. Private homes on Cyprus dating to the nineteenth and early twentieth centuries display many characteristics of Turkish architecture. Nicosia has two Ottoman caravanserai (caravan trading inns) dating from the sixteenth century.

Recreation and Food

The mild climate and extensive coastline of Cyprus allow a wide range of water sports and other recreations. Swimming, sailing, and diving are popular in the Mediterranean Sea. Hiking, camping, and skiing are possible in the mountains of the interior. Many hotels and seaside resorts have tennis courts and Olympic-sized pools. Sports clubs sponsor recreational and amateur teams. Since independence in 1960, the two states on Cyprus have built additional stadiums and sports halls.

A major event on the European auto-racing circuit is the 72-hour Cyprus Rally, which is held each September. Greek Cypriots also send small teams to the Olympic Games, which originated in Greece more than 2,000 years ago. In 1989 Cyprus hosted the Games of the Small Countries of Europe, in which eight other nations participated.

The cuisine of Cyprus is closely related to that of mainland Greece, Turkey, and the Middle East. Most Cypriots eat a light breakfast, then have lunch in the early afternoon. The evening meal, the largest of the day, begins around 9 or 10 P.M. This meal can last for hours and is often an occasion for large gatherings of family and friends. The first course, a plate of appetizers, may include *tzadziki*, a mixture of yogurt and fresh cucumber, or an eggplant salad. Popular soups include *avgholemono*, or egg-lemon soup. Lentil and chickpea soup are also common.

Main meals may consist of fish or meat dishes, salads, casseroles, and fresh vegetables. Moussaka is a mixture of baked ground beef and spices, layered between slices of eggplant. *Stifado* is beef or veal stew, often spiced with wild herbs. Lamb, the most popular meat course, may be grilled on skewers as souvlaki (*kebab* in

Photo © Andrew E. Beswick

A skier glides down a slope in the Troodos Mountains. Seasonal snow and mild temperatures create ideal skiing conditions in this range.

Neighborhood coffeehouses draw patrons for food, refreshments, and conversation.

Photo by M. L. Verhoef, the Netherlands

Turkish) or cooked in a pot with vegetables and spices as *tavas.* Cooks also grill or bake swordfish, mullet, and red snapper. Mussels, shrimp, and lobster are favorite shellfish. Beans, potatoes, zucchini, and eggplant are popular vegetables on Cyprus.

Traditional Cypriot desserts include baklava and *kataifi,* pastries made with honey syrup. *Loukoumi,* or Turkish delight, is a sweet, edible gum dusted with powdered sugar. *Loukoumades* are sweet doughnuts dipped in syrup. Cypriots can also choose from a wide variety of fruit grown on the island, including melons, cherries, peaches, oranges, plums, figs, and grapes.

Cypriots drink tea or sweet, thick coffee for breakfast and after meals. Southern Cyprus produces white, red, and rosé wines, as well as beer and brandy. Commandaria is a famous red dessert wine from Cyprus. Ouzo (*raki* in Turkish), an anise-flavored liqueur, is enjoyed by some adults as a before-dinner drink.

Baklava—a layered pastry made with walnuts and honey—is a favorite dessert on Cyprus.

Courtesy of Cultural and Tourism Office of the Turkish Embassy

49

A fisherman maneuvers his catch toward a dock. Cypriot crews haul in about 3,000 tons of fish every year.

4) The Economy

The economy of Cyprus suffered a sharp decline after the violent conflicts of 1974. The fighting drove more than 200,000 Greek and Turkish refugees from their homes. In addition, farms were damaged and many factories destroyed in northern Cyprus. Tourism—a thriving industry and an important source of earnings—nearly ceased. With the physical division of the island, the Republic of Cyprus also lost access to important resources in northern Cyprus.

Careful government planning and foreign aid from Britain, Greece, and international organizations brought about a gradual recovery in southern Cyprus in the late 1970s. Manufacturing replaced agriculture as the largest sector of the economy. Export earnings rose as prosperous, oil-rich countries in the Middle East became trading partners.

In the 1980s, as the island's political situation stabilized, foreign investment increased in southern Cyprus. To escape civil conflict in Lebanon, some Lebanese businesses moved to the port cities of Larnaca and Limassol. Telecommunications and shipping industries contributed to the area's economic growth. The most serious problem now faced by companies in southern Cyprus is a shortage of skilled labor.

In northern Cyprus, however, economic recovery has proceeded much more slowly. The 1974 conflict left the area with damaged cities, a decrease in foreign trade, and a shortage of skilled and unskilled labor. In addition, an international trade embargo sharply restricted exports from northern Cyprus. The Turkish Cypriots attempted to integrate their economy with that of Turkey, a country with serious economic problems of its own. Since only Turkey recognizes the Turkish Republic of Northern Cyprus, few foreign businesses will trade or invest in the area.

Courtesy of Embassy of the Republic of Cyprus

To increase the number of experienced laborers in southern Cyprus, the government sponsors classes in industrial skills *(above)* **and in computer programming** *(below)* **at vocational schools.**

Courtesy of Embassy of the Republic of Cyprus

51

In the early 1990s, agriculture remained the mainstay of northern Cyprus's economy. High unemployment and inflation persisted, and income per person was one-third that of southern Cyprus. Limited investment and trade bans on goods from northern Cyprus continue to hamper growth. Although northern Cyprus receives some aid and investment from Turkey, its economy is stagnant.

Manufacturing

Accounting for about 25 percent of total production, manufacturing has replaced agriculture as the chief economic activity in southern Cyprus. Factories in the region make clothing, shoes, chemicals, and machinery. Other plants produce cement, bricks, and tiles for the construction industry. The processing of food and beverages provides both employment and export income.

Most small companies in southern Cyprus still focus on less profitable, traditional goods. Many older factories use inefficient methods of production, and Cypriot manufacturers must import many of the needed raw materials.

In the early 1990s, the government encouraged companies in southern Cyprus to make a wider range of products in order to increase exports. The government invested in new factories that were designed to assemble specialized, high-technology electronic goods. This type of manufacturing, however, demands a large and skilled labor force. Cyprus also faces stiff competition from similar businesses in Europe and in Asia.

Agriculture

The 1974 fighting on Cyprus forced many farmers from their land. The conflict reduced the amount of land used for raising crops. In addition, livestock production fell by 50 percent.

In the Republic of Cyprus, modernization programs brought about a gradual

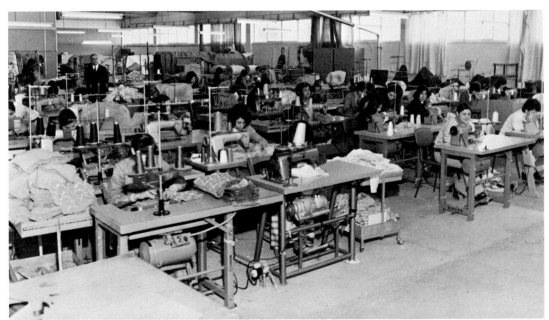

Textile workers manufacture clothing at a factory in southern Cyprus. The clothing industry is a major employer and accounts for a high percentage of Cypriot exports.

Sheep graze on pastureland near Kyrenia. In recent years, farmers have raised the quality of livestock through improved breeding, up-to-date veterinary care, and better nutrition.

recovery in agriculture. Irrigation projects have helped crops to survive the severe droughts that occur in the region. About half of the land in southern Cyprus is now under cultivation, and new dams and canal systems bring a steady supply of water to 15 percent of these acreages. Nearly half of the population works in agriculture, but farming and livestock raising contribute only about 10 percent of the country's total production of goods.

The principal livestock raised on Cyprus are cattle, sheep, goats, pigs, and poultry. In some areas, semi-nomadic herders move their flocks of sheep and goats between the mountain valleys and lowland plains. Farmers breed quails, rabbits, and pigeons to sell on the domestic market.

Courtesy of F. Mattioli/FAO

A farmer threshes hay that will be used as animal feed. Little rain falls on Cyprus during the summer months, but crop production continues to rise as Cypriots build new irrigation systems.

Farmers in low-lying valleys plant cereal crops, such as wheat and barley. Potatoes, an important export crop, and other vegetables grow throughout the island. Barley and potatoes are also key crops in northern Cyprus. Citrus and olive trees thrive along the seacoasts, and Cypriot farmers harvest carob, an edible bean that comes from a common Mediterranean evergreen. Farmers take advantage of the milder climate in the mountain valleys to grow fruit trees, nut trees, and grapevines.

Photo © Andrew E. Beswick

Fruit pickers empty their baskets of recently harvested oranges. Cyprus produces more than 160 tons of citrus fruit every year.

Trade

Because Cyprus must import most of its raw materials, international trade is vital to the Cypriot economy. In addition, the island's domestic market is too small to absorb all of its finished products. Cyprus has established a customs union with the European Community (EC), a trade association of European nations. This arrangement lowers import duties on many products bought and sold between Cyprus and the EC countries. In 1990 the Republic of Cyprus made a formal application to join the EC. The island's admission depends on a resolution of the continuing political conflict between Greek and Turkish Cypriots.

Once part of the British Empire, Cyprus still carries out most of its foreign trade with Britain. Germany and Japan also export to Cyprus. To broaden the country's overseas market, both regions of Cyprus are attempting to expand commercial links with the nations of the Middle East. Most industrial companies on Cyprus now export their goods to Middle Eastern states. Despite its expanding economy, southern Cyprus has a trade deficit, meaning that the republic spends more money to import goods than it earns from the sale of its exports.

The island's most important agricultural exports are citrus fruits, potatoes, and wine. Manufacturing exports include clothing and footwear. Without energy resources of its own, Cyprus must import its oil, most of which comes from the Middle East. Earnings from tourism and money sent home by Cypriots working abroad account for most of the foreign currency earned by southern Cyprus.

Northern Cyprus, which trades with both Turkey and the EC countries, mainly exports food and textiles. Northern Cyprus must import oil, machinery, and transportation equipment. Few foreign companies, however, have set up business ties with the north.

Workers at the port of Limassol prepare to load goods onto a waiting ship. The island's location near major sea-lanes has enabled Cyprus to expand its foreign trade.

Photo © Andrew E. Beswick

The decreasing amount of copper reserves in Cyprus forced this mine and others in the northern region to close.

World Bank Photo

A worker dangles from a high ladder while repairing a power line near Larnaca.

Mining and Energy

In ancient times, copper mining was an important activity on Cyprus and made the island a center of Mediterranean trade. Over the centuries, reserves of this mineral gradually declined as miners exhausted the supply of copper ore. Most of the island's copper mines eventually closed, and copper and other minerals currently make up only 2 percent of the total value of exports from southern Cyprus. The most important minerals now include asbestos, chromite, iron pyrites, and bentonite, an absorbent clay used to make paper and medicines.

Since the 1950s, nearly all towns and villages on Cyprus have installed electrical service. Rapid population growth and the expansion of the island's economy brought about a sharp increase in energy demand in the 1970s and 1980s. To generate power, however, Cyprus must import large amounts of the oil needed to fuel three

Construction workers *(left)* struggle with electric cable that will be laid at a new power station near Limassol. Most electricity on Cyprus is produced from imported crude oil, which is brought to refineries for processing *(below)*.

Tourists who make the long climb to the Temple of Apollo are rewarded with a view of the ancient sanctuary of Apollo Hylates. Dating to A.D. 100, the sanctuary stands at the edge of the ancient city of Kourion.

Photo © Andrew E. Beswick

large power plants. The government of southern Cyprus is planning a new coal-fired power plant on the southern coast.

The ministry that controls electricity production on Cyprus continues to provide electric service to homes and businesses in northern Cyprus. In order to ease dependence on electricity from the south, two hydroelectric plants are under construction by the agency that controls electric distribution in northern Cyprus.

Tourism

Cyprus was once a favorite destination for tourists from Britain, many of whom established second homes on the island. But tourism, like other sectors of the economy, suffered greatly from the civil conflict of the 1970s. Most tourist facilities in northern Cyprus were closed after 1974, and ongoing violence and turmoil discouraged visitors for several years thereafter.

In the late 1970s and 1980s, developers in southern Cyprus built new hotels, resorts, and other vacation facilities. Tourists gradually returned to enjoy the island's mild climate and cultural attractions, and tourism was an important part of the south's economic recovery. In the early 1990s, tourism became the largest source of foreign income in southern Cyprus.

Founded by the Lusignans in the thirteenth century, Bellapais Abbey — also known as the Abbey of Peace — attracts visitors with its elaborate architecture and beautifully carved interior. Perched on a cliff near Kyrenia, the abbey overlooks the village of Bellapais as well as groves of cypress, palm, orange, and olive trees.

Photo © Andrew E. Beswick

Photo © Andrew E. Beswick

Kyrenia lights up at night, drawing tourists to the restaurants and meeting places that line the harbor.

The bright blue waters of the Mediterranean break against the long, sandy beaches that surround the island.

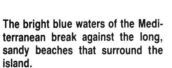

Photo © Andrew E. Beswick

59

Most visitors to southern Cyprus are from Britain, Norway, Sweden, Denmark, Germany, Greece, and Lebanon. About one million tourists arrive each year. Popular destinations include archaeological sites and beachfront resorts. The monasteries of the Troodos Mountains draw both religious pilgrims and tourists. A brief winter season allows skiing on Mount Olympus, and horseback riding and hiking are also popular in the forests of the Troodos Mountains.

Tourism is the largest source of foreign earnings in northern Cyprus, which draws the majority of its visitors from Turkey. Beaches and quiet villages attract many of these tourists, and the Kyrenia Mountains are the site of impressive medieval fortifications and castles.

Transportation

The Attila Line prevents almost all movement between northern and southern Cyprus. Cypriots may not cross the line, and foreign visitors must make a special application to travel between the two sectors by land or sea.

A system of paved, two-lane roads connects most towns and villages on Cyprus. A newer, four-lane freeway links the capital of Nicosia with the port of Limassol.

Photo by M. Ergün Olgun

The castle of Kyrenia looms at the entrance to the old port city. Dating to the thirteenth century, the castle's massive walls enclose a chapel, prison cells, and dungeons.

World Bank Photo

Investment in new roads and harbors has helped Cyprus build its important trade economy. Road crews *(left)* pave this new highway between Nicosia and Larnaca, which opened in 1991. The largest port on Cyprus, Limassol *(below)* was built in the mid-1970s. More than 5,000 vessels dock at the island's port facilities every year.

Courtesy of Embassy of the Republic of Cyprus

Since vehicles and fuel must be imported and are expensive, many Cypriots use buses to travel around the island. No railroad lines exist on Cyprus.

Limassol and Larnaca, the chief ports of southern Cyprus, shelter both cargo ships and passenger vessels. Kyrenia is a small fishing port on the northern coast of Cyprus. Famagusta, once the island's busiest port, closed as a commercial harbor after the Turkish invasion of 1974. Greek Cypriots working in the port fled, and shipping businesses moved to southern Cyprus.

The division of Cyprus also closed the island's main international airport at Nicosia. Most international flights now arrive at Larnaca. A smaller airfield exists near Paphos, which serves western Cyprus.

61

The limited-access highway between Nicosia and Limassol has been open since 1985. Road development has increased in recent years to meet the needs of new industries and to stimulate tourism.

Courtesy of Embassy of the Republic of Cyprus

The Future

Although southern Cyprus has recovered from the 1974 conflict, northern Cyprus still suffers high unemployment and a lower standard of living. Efforts to develop industry and to modernize agriculture in northern Cyprus have not always been successful. It will be difficult to attract new investment to the region unless

Courtesy of Embassy of the Republic of Cyprus

About 30 international airlines service Larnaca Airport, the largest airfield on Cyprus.

Photo © Andrew E. Beswick

Turkish Cypriots and Greek Cypriots can resolve their differences and reintegrate the island's economy.

In the early 1990s, a solution to the political and military stalemate on Cyprus seemed unlikely. Greek and Turkish Cypriots cannot agree on the status of Turkish military forces, on claims on property lost during the 1974 conflict, or on a form of government. Although leaders in Greece and Turkey have tried to end the island's division, the historic feud between these two nations has prevented successful negotiation.

Index

Africa, 7, 21, 27
Agriculture, 10, 20, 25, 29–30, 32, 40, 50, 52–55, 62. *See also* Citrus fruit; Livestock; Potatoes; Wine
Air travel, 18, 61–62
Akrotiri Bay, 12, 17
Akrotiri Peninsula, 12–13
Alexander the Great, 24
Andreas, Cape, 10–11
Arabs, 27
Archaeological sites, 20–21, 45–46, 60
Architecture, 16–17, 46–47, 59
Arts, 21, 40, 45–47
Asbestos, 15–16, 56
Asia Minor, 7, 20–24, 29–30, 39. *See also* Turkey
Assyria, 7, 22
Athens, 23
Attila Line, 36, 38–39, 60
Bellapais Abbey, 59
Byzantine Empire, 26–27, 29, 44–46
Cathedral of Santa Sophia (Selimiye Mosque), 17, 41
Christianity, 7, 24–25, 27, 45–46
Chromite, 15–16, 56
Cities, 16–19. *See also* Famagusta; Larnaca; Limassol; Nicosia; Paphos
Citrus fruit, 54–55
Civil conflict, 35–37
Climate, 12–14, 54
Clothing industry, 17, 52, 55
Constantinople (Istanbul), 26, 27, 29
Copper, 15–16, 20, 56
Crusaders, 18–19, 27–29
Cyprus
  boundaries, size, and location of, 10
  flag of, 34
  independence of, 34–37
  population of, 39–40
Cyprus, Church of, 40
Cyprus, University of, 43
Denktash, Raouf, 38
Dhiarizos River, 12
Eastern Roman Empire. *See* Byzantine Empire
Eastern Orthodox Church, 8, 27, 29–30, 40, 44, 46
Economy, 9, 20, 50–63
Education, 43, 51
Egypt, 7, 21–22, 24, 29, 31
Elections, 36–38
Energy, 55–58
Episkopi Bay, 12
Europe, 7, 9, 21–22, 24–25, 27, 29, 31, 33, 43, 55
European Community (EC), 55
Exports, 16, 18, 20–22, 50–52, 54–56
Ezouza River, 12
Famagusta, 13, 17–19, 27, 29, 36, 38, 61
Famagusta Bay, 13
Festivals, 8, 40–41
Feudalism, 29–30
Fishing, 20, 50, 61
Flora and Fauna, 14–15
Food, 48–49
Foreign aid, 50–51
Forests and Forestry, 14–15, 43
France, 33

Gata, Cape, 12
Genoa, 29
Germany, 33, 55
Government, 9, 34–35, 38, 43, 63
Great Britain, 8, 17, 31–35, 50, 55, 58
Greece, 7–10, 18, 20–22, 29, 31–34, 36, 48, 50, 62–63
Greek Cypriots, 7–9, 16–17, 22–24, 30–40, 48, 55, 63
Green Line, 36
Health, 42
History, 7–9, 20–38
  Byzantine Empire, 26–28
  civil conflict and division, 35–38
  early settlements, 20–24
  independence, 33–37
  Lusignan dynasty, 28–29
  Ottoman Empire, 29–33
  Roman rule, 20, 24–26
  twentieth century, 32–38
Holidays, 40–41
House of Representatives, 34–35, 38
Hunting, 7, 15, 20
Hydroelectric power, 58
Imports, 52, 55–56, 61
Industry, 17–19, 50–52, 62
Infant mortality, 42
Irrigation, 10–11, 14, 53–54
Islam, 7, 27–28, 30, 41, 46
Italian Peninsula, 7, 17, 24, 29
Japan, 55
Judicial system, 38
Karpas Peninsula, 10–11
Kato Pyrgos, 36
Kourion, 21, 25, 44–45, 58
Kuchuk, Fazil, 35
Kyprianou, Spyros, 37
Kyrenia, 5, 11, 16, 38, 53, 59–61
Kyrenia Mountains, 5, 11–12, 14, 28, 40, 60
Lakes, 13
Land, 10–19
Languages, 44
Larnaca, 11, 13, 15–16, 18, 27, 29, 51, 61–62
Larnaca Bay, 12, 18
Lausanne, Treaty of, 33
Lebanon, 7, 39–40, 51
Life expectancy, 42
Limassol, 8, 12, 15–18, 27, 29, 51, 55, 57, 60–62
Literature, 44–45
Livestock, 52–53, 55
Lusignan dynasty, 28–29, 45–46, 59
Makarios, Archbishop (Mikhail Khristodolou Mouskas), 8, 33–37
Manufacturing, 50, 52, 55
Maps, 6, 11
Maronite Christians, 40
Mediterranean Sea, 5, 7, 10, 12–13, 21–22, 24–25, 27, 29, 31–32, 42, 48, 59, 62
Mesaoria Plain, 10–13, 17, 20, 40
Middle East, 7, 17, 18, 20–25, 27–29, 31, 39, 42, 48, 51, 55
Mining, 15–16, 20, 56
Morphou Bay, 11, 13, 16, 36
Morphou Plain, 11, 14, 20, 40
Mosques, 27, 31–32, 46
Mycenaeans, 7, 18
National Assembly, 38
Natural resources, 15–16

Nea Paphos, 24–25
Nicosia, 10, 13–14, 16–17, 27–29, 31, 35–36, 39–41, 47, 60–63
Northern Cyprus, 8–10, 14, 16–19, 36–39, 41, 43, 50–52, 54–55, 58, 60–62
Northern Cyprus, Turkish Republic of, 37, 41, 51
Oil, 55–57
Old Paphos, 7, 19
Olympic Games, 48
Olympus, Mount, 11, 14, 60
Ottoman Empire, 29–33, 45
Ottoman Turks, 7, 17–18, 29–31, 41, 46
Ovgos River, 13
Palea Paphos, 19, 21
Paphos, 11, 19, 22, 45–46, 61
Pedieas River, 13
People, 39–49
  education, 43, 51
  health, 42
  language, 44
  religion, 7, 40–41
Persia, 7, 23
Petra tou Romiou, 7
Philosophy, 44
Phoenicians, 7, 18, 22–23
Plakos River, 13
Population, 16, 40
Ports, 5, 7–8, 11, 17–19, 22, 26, 61. *See also* Famagusta; Larnaca; Limassol; Paphos
Potatoes, 54–55
Ptolemaic kings, 24
Rainfall, 13
Recreation, 48
Reforestation, 14
Refugees, 9, 16–18, 21, 37–40, 42, 50, 63
Resorts, 11, 17–19, 58, 60
Rhodes, 10
Richard the Lion-Hearted, 28
Rivers, 10, 12–13
Roads and highways, 15–16, 60–62
Roman Catholic Church, 27–30, 40–41
Roman Empire, 7, 17, 24–27
Rome, 24, 26–27
Russia, 31–33
Salamis, 13, 19–21, 23–25, 44–45
Sampson, Nikos, 36
Sculpture, 45
Serakhis River, 13
Shipping, 21, 51, 55, 61
Soloi, 10, 45
Southern Cyprus, 8–9, 14, 17, 37–38, 40, 43, 50–53, 55–56, 58–62
Standard of living, 42, 62
Syria, 10, 24, 26–27
Temple of Apollo, 58
Timber, 20–21, 24
Topography, 10–12
Tourism, 9, 17–19, 50, 55, 58–60
Trade, 10, 15–16, 18, 20–22, 24, 27, 30, 32, 51–52, 55–56
Transportation, 18, 60–62
Troodos Mountains, 11–15, 20, 40, 48, 60
Turkey, 7–10, 31–38, 48, 51, 52, 55, 60, 63. *See also* Asia Minor
Turkish Cypriots, 8–9, 16–17, 30, 32–39, 41, 51, 55, 63

Tyre, 23–24, 28
Unemployment, 52, 62
United Nations, 9, 34–37
United States, 38, 43
Vassiliou, George, 37–38
Venice, 29–30, 47
Voting rights, 38
Western Roman Empire, 26, 44
Wine, 18, 49, 55
World War I, 33
World War II, 33
Zeno, 44